GET RECRUITED THROUGH LINKEDIN

Creating Your Personal Brand and Finding a Job using

LinkedIn

Tejas Subrahmanya

Surajaya Consultants

© 2015

Disclaimer

The information provided in this book is designed to provide helpful information on the subjects discussed. The publisher and author are not responsible and liable for any damages or negative consequences from any action, to any person reading or following the information provided in this book. This book has been written to provide guidelines on the topic of reference, and not to be construed as the absolute truth. Readers are advised to exercise their discretion while applying the concepts descried in the book. References are provided for informational purposes only and do not constitute endorsement of any websites or other sources. Readers should be aware that the website listed in this book may change.

While attempts have been made to verify that the information contained in this publication is accurate, neither the author nor the publisher assumes any responsibility for errors, omissions, interpretations or usage of the subject matters herein. This publication contains the opinions and ideas of its author and is intended for informational purposes only. The author and publisher shall in no event be held liable for any loss or other damages incurred the usage of the publication.

Table of Contents

Chapter 1 – Introduction

There are many ways for you to search for jobs today. As you will read through this book, you will find that there are a number of platforms available to you for searching for jobs.

As readers, I know that you would be aware of various platforms for searching for jobs, but my aim was not to highlight the platforms per se, but to let you know that there are a number of platforms are available and you are free to choose the one you think is best for you.

However, the focus of this book will be on how you can use LinkedIn to search for a job.

I will be covering concepts on how to create a good LinkedIn Profile, the features of a good profile, developing a personal brand in LinkedIn, linking your LinkedIn profile with your offline resume, publishing your thought leadership, endorsing and recommending people in your network (and in the process, you receive endorsements and recommendations), following companies and keeping yourself updated about the latest developments taking place in your circle and interest groups.

During the course of reading the book, you will also understand the do's and don'ts of maintaining a LinkedIn profile, and how you can make your profile effective by following simple rules of thumb, that I have described in the chapter on Do's and Don'ts.

To make matters simpler, you will a number of practical examples that you can use. These examples reinforce what you should be doing to ensure that your brand on the LinkedIn Community stands out.

You will also read a section on what recruiters look for in candidates when they use LinkedIn Recruiter, a tool for recruiters. The book starts with what recruiters look for from a LinkedIn profile because I believe that if you know what recruiters look for, it will be easy for you to tailor make your profile to suit their requirements.

While this book is definitely useful for beginners, I believe this will be useful for people who have been maintaining their profile with LinkedIn for the past several years.

You will find me repeating some points very often but I believe this is really required here. LinkedIn is a networking platform. You will have to shift your focus from you to others. This is not a typical job portal where you focus only on your achievements and your progress. While this is important, it is also important that you value your network, and leverage the people in your network for your benefit.

When you leverage them for your benefit, you need to focus on the long term, and keep in touch with them, congratulate them, wish them on their marriage anniversaries and birthdays, and show to them that they are an important part of your life.

As you will read through the book, you will also understand that it is important for you to indicate that even after you have got a job through your strong referral network that you value your contacts.

It takes years to build your network, but seconds to destroy it. Never let this happen to you. If you are in the network to fulfill your self-serving biases, then this is probably not the space for you to be in. You will be wasting your time, as well as those of your network, and it will take no time for the contacts in your network to "Unconnect" you from their list.

With these precautions, I urge you to read this book thoroughly, and put into practice what has been displayed. I am sure it will help you go a long way in achieving your goals and objectives, especially if you are seeking to join a company of your choice.

Happy Reading!!!

Chapter 2 – Platforms to Search for Jobs

When I was pursuing my Master's in Business Administration, I learnt that there are a number of sources for recruiting candidates. Let me take some time to explain these sources, because these sources form the platforms that you will use for searching jobs. However, today, the very relevance of these sources seem to be threatened, thanks to LinkedIn. Before we proceed to understanding how LinkedIn has influenced the way recruiters recruit, let us understand some very basic concepts.

Recruitment is the process that focuses on soliciting resumes from prospective candidates for vacant positions in an organization.

I have been very closely involved in the recruitment process of companies. Whenever I have had to solicit candidates for vacant positions in the organization I worked for, I have resorted to soliciting resumes from prospective candidates.

This is in contrast to selection methods; I should rather use the term rejection methods, because once you are shortlisted by the concerned HR department, you are required to go through a series of steps that results in the elimination of unfit candidates from the pool of candidates.

The final step in the rejection process is the actual selection of the candidate(s) who fit into the organizational set up.

With this brief background about the concept of recruitment and selection (rejection), let me proceed to help you understand the platforms that are available for you to search for jobs. These platforms are the same sources that recruiters use for soliciting your resumes.

"Choose a job you love, and you will never have to work a day in your life" - Confucius

A number of recruiters and employers tend to use the recruiting yield pyramid to calculate the number of applicants they need to solicit for hiring candidates against the vacant positions in their organization.

Let me help you understand this with the help of an example.

You want to apply to an engineer's position at GE Power in Vietnam, and you find that the employer wants to hire 30 such candidates with experience similar to what you have. You want to be among the 30 candidates to be selected for the vacant positions in the company.

So, the recruiter at GE Power in Vietnam makes a small calculation and prepares a pyramid as given below. From experience, the recruiter knows that:

1. The ratio of offers made to actual new hires is 2:1
2. The ratio of candidates interviewed to offers made is 3:2
3. The ratio of candidates invited for interviews to candidates actually interviewed is 4:3
4. Finally, only 1 candidate out of 5 leads generated gets invited for an interview.

The Recruiting Yield Pyramid will now look like this.

Fig. 1: Recruiting Yield Pyramid
Source: Gary Dessler & Biju Varkkey, HRM, 11th Ed., Pg. 179, Pearson Education

So, you see from the above pyramid, if you need to get selected for this position, you have to compete with about 600 candidates, who would have applied from various sources to the company's vacant positions.

How would you want to apply to such a position, which you feel is relevant to you?

You can apply through one of the following methods for various vacant positions in these organizations.

1. Via the Internet, using job portals as well as company websites
2. Through ads placed in newspapers
3. Using Employment and Temp Agencies
4. Executive Recruiters
5. College Recruiters
6. Referrals and Walk-Ins

I know you are well versed in these platforms, and you may be using one or more of them for your job search. My focus is not to explain these platforms, but to give you an idea of how LinkedIn has been influencing these platforms.

Via Internet: Job portals and company websites.
This is one of the most common methods for people to access vacancies across companies, and probably the most popular. One survey recently identified that more than 4 million people turn to the Internet, searching for jobs. It has been found that most employers find it easier to post requirements on job portals like Monster.com, Indeed.com, JobsAhead.com, and others. If you have the right profile and are able to include the right mix of your experience and academic qualifications, recruiters can find your profile easily using keyword search for experience, location and qualifications.

The problem with many of these websites is that you can only search for jobs, unlike **LinkedIn** where you can create your network. The job portals are mostly meant for prospective candidates to search for jobs at short notice or want to reach out to a large number of companies quickly.

I predict that a day will come when even job portals will start seeking the services of LinkedIn for placing candidates for jobs in various companies. While many third party recruiters, like employment agencies and search firms have lost their market or are set to lose their market to LinkedIn, a time will come when even job portals will have to depend on LinkedIn for their overall sustenance.

In addition to the above mentioned portals where companies can post their requirements, they also have a career page on their respective websites for soliciting resumes from prospective candidates.

However, most companies today prefer to use the LinkedIn Platform to solicit resumes from prospective candidates. Companies have found that there are a number of advantages of using the LinkedIn Platform for recruiting.

A recruiter from any company, who has created a company profile on LinkedIn can post jobs and search for candidates. I will explain more about how recruiters can find candidates in the next chapter.

If you visit any company's website, you will find that they have a profile associated with LinkedIn and Facebook, and you can follow and like them, respectively.

Ads in Print Media
Ads in print media, while still being popular, are also going the LinkedIn way. In most advertisements of companies, and you will find links to their LinkedIn and Facebook Profiles.

What this means for you is that you can also visit their LinkedIn, Facebook, and other social networking Profiles for additional information.

This also indicates that companies are now using LinkedIn and other social networking sites to reach out to prospective candidates even while adopting a multi-pronged recruitment approach.

Using Employment and Temp Agencies

Employment and temp Agencies have lost their sheen since the introduction of the LinkedIn way of recruiting candidates. While many employment agencies have lost steam, they do seem to find opportunities especially with smaller organizations that need help in identifying candidates.

LinkedIn has actually eaten into the recruitment industry in a big way. In an article written on Oct 24, 2012, author Marc Andreesen argues that the recruitment industry will see two groups emerging – the innovators and the ostriches. And the harbinger for this emergence would be LinkedIn.

And this prediction is not without any reason. Over the last few years, LinkedIn has replaced the role of the traditional third party recruiter. With every new feature that LinkedIn got into its kitty, the traditional recruiter got relegated to the background.

It has now become the case of the "disruptor beating the incumbent." One of the most important and critical asset that third party recruiters had was their network of candidates. This was their secret sauce for helping companies hire talent from across the country, and probably the world too.

Today, this secret sauce has been thrown into the open by LinkedIn, and the role of the traditional recruiter has minimized. Instead, recruiters from companies are finding it easier to use LinkedIn's built-in talent management solutions to hire talent to their organizations.

LinkedIn's owes its success story to contribution of recruiters of various companies. Consider these facts, and you will understand what I mean.

1. Companies turn to external recruiters for two reasons
   a. To access talent they cannot access themselves
   b. Outsource the recruitment process
2. LinkedIn has disrupted both these reasons for companies to go to external recruiters

      a.   LinkedIn has democratized the access to talent

      b.   With its state-of-the-art products like Talent Pipeline and LinkedIn Recruiter, companies are learning to bypass the external recruiter

3. However, 93% of external recruiters were hooked on to LinkedIn for recruitment in 2012, up from 78% the previous year, 2011

4. External recruiters themselves are being increasingly dependent on LinkedIn for a database. Thus, a proprietary database that they owned and operated is no longer a prerequisite to get them hooked on to a company

5. Pfizer reported that 40% of all their hires came through LinkedIn

6. Accenture plans to hire 40% of its 50,000 strong new hires through LinkedIn and Twitter

Consider this statement from LinkedIn from their 2011 S1 Statement:

"We believe our solutions are both more cost effective and more efficient than traditional recruiting solutions, such as hiring third-party search firms, to identify and screen candidates."

The author goes on to add that there would be two sets of companies competing with each other for supremacy.

1. Innovators: those groups who understand that they cannot live without LinkedIn and adapt themselves to the new scenario and adopt newer business models, invest heavily in technology, and social media, which employers may not be able to do, and drive innovation in recruitment and processes

2. Ostriches: would still stick to the age old practices, arguing in blogs and conferences about their "rights as professional recruiters", and sticking their head in the sand and saying, "Everything is OK!"

Today, the odds are that as a candidate, you may be hired through LinkedIn than any other platform, and you will never have to go to a third-party recruiter. Even if you get hired by a third party recruiter, you would invariably be tracked through your LinkedIn profile, and this will be the universal truth a few years down the line.

Whether you will seek a full time employment or a temporary assignment with a number of employers, you will have only one profile, your LinkedIn Profile, and this will be the only thing that will matter. You need not approach various firms for showcasing your resume and requesting them to get you placed in a company.

Executive Recruiters
Executive search firms are in a state of flux now. The pride of all executive search firms is their up-to-date database of the world's C-level executives. And this makes the executive recruiters very sought after property by these executives.

As an executive, you are also very particular about the firm with which you are sharing your details with. Confidentiality, authenticity and reputation are some of the key factors that you would look for in an executive search firm.

With many executives also having their profiles on LinkedIn, and being part of a network of nearly half a billion people, the database of the executive search firm is under threat.

Probably the only reason why executive search firms have been immune from the onslaught of LinkedIn is that they provide a more humane touch to the entire process of recruiting C-level executives. One thing that nobody does in LinkedIn is give a negative comment about anyone. However, an executive search consultant would look at a person from both sides of a coin, getting to know areas where he/she has been negatively evaluated as well as his/her strengths. For e.g. executive search consultants can figure out if a particular C-level executive was involved in any sexual harassment case, whereas comments on such topics are generally avoided in the LinkedIn forum.

To this extent, executive search firms have been isolated, but the day will not be far when someone new or an existing executive search firm will use the LinkedIn database to recruit C-level executives, while still managing to weigh the pros and cons of hiring such an individual to a company, ensuring that the individual fits into the organization culturally and from a personality perspective.

Executive search firms will not be able to keep themselves immune to the LinkedIn database, and at some point in time, they will have to adopt to the changed scenario. I expect executive search firms to split into two groups – the Innovators and the Ostriches, as described in the previous section on employment and temp agencies.

College Recruiters
The biggest change that LinkedIn will bring about is in the recruitment of college graduates.

With LinkedIn's advanced search abilities, recruiters need not physically visit colleges and get in touch with the placement/career services directors for recruiting college graduates. They can rather search for college graduates in LinkedIn, focus on those who have a specific grade, from a specific stream, have interned in a specific company and have undertaken a specific project that is relevant to their firm.

Through LinkedIn, recruiters have access to a large number college graduates, from different colleges and universities. For a recruiter, this is a boon, because he/she need not visit a college/university physically, and on the click of a button, get the output of their search criteria.

Potentially, LinkedIn can reduce the cost of recruiting college graduates by up to 80%. Once they shortlist a college graduate for their organization, they can organize online tests, arrange for a Skype interview and finally call them for a face-to-face interview.

The role Career Services Director/Placement Director changes drastically, and he/she no longer needs to contact recruiters of companies, but would rather focus on ensuring that the students' LinkedIn profile is as impressive as possible. The Career Services Director will receive a new designation/position – **Director of LinkedIn Services**

Referrals

Employee referrals has received the greatest boost through LinkedIn. Employees working in an organization can now use LinkedIn to refer candidate who they feel is a good fit.

If you know a colleague from your school/college/university working in a company of your choice, you can always send him/her a mail, requesting to forward the details to the concerned recruiter.

Most companies find that referral is the most reliable means of recruiting candidates as there is some degree of credibility about the candidate being referred to.

LinkedIn has made it possible to a considerable extent, and is the most preferred method of recruiting people in many organizations.

Chapter 3 – LinkedIn for Recruitment

In the previous chapter I described how LinkedIn has been influencing the way you use various platforms for applying to companies and getting a job.

Let us now move forward and take time to focus on the concept that I have been trying to drive home – LinkedIn Job Search.

I am sure many of you have an account with LinkedIn, a very popular social networking website. LinkedIn is the world's largest professional networking website, with over 300 million members from over 200 countries and territories.

The Mission of LinkedIn is to:

"Connect the world's professionals to make them more productive and successful. When you join LinkedIn, you get access to people, jobs, news, updates and insights that help you be great at what you do."

LinkedIn started off from the living room of co-founder Reid Hoffman in 2002, and was officially launched on May 5th, 2003.

It is a publicly listed company, with revenues generated from member subscriptions, advertising sales and talent solutions.

Well, you may be wondering why I am describing what LinkedIn is and its use in this book. You can always visit the website and get the information you want.

I have a specific reason why I have included this here. If I

"Talent hits a target no one else can hit; genius hits a target no one else can see" – Arthur Schopenhauer

assume that you are reading this book, I don't think you will go back and open a browser and visit www.linkedin.com/about-us?trk=hp-about to understand about LinkedIn. So, what I have presented is something that is quite relevant to what we will discuss further in this book, and this book is all about searching jobs using LinkedIn.

Whether you have created an account with LinkedIn, or you are yet to create one, what I am going to describe below will help you for the rest of your career, and possibly your life too.

Let us recall the mission for LinkedIn. As a member of LinkedIn, you get access to jobs, people, news, updates and insights that will help you be great at what you are and what you do.

This indicates that LinkedIn is a platform for you to get linked professionally, and show how strong your professional network is. In addition, you can search for jobs that are posted on LinkedIn; you can also provide showcase your thought leadership by providing updates and insights that indicate the kind of person you are.

Before the Internet became ubiquitous, I keep wondering how people did their business, hired people and followed articles on thought leadership.

With a platform like LinkedIn one can do a variety of things so easily. I believe the future of recruitment will be through LinkedIn, and probably Facebook too, and other similar professional and social networking sites.

There various ways in which you can take advantage of the LinkedIn platform to enable your search for the right job, and prove that you have the ability in you to do great things.

LinkedIn also provides solutions to companies, like talent solutions. Understanding what these solutions mean is very important for you so that you can tailor make your profile and make it stand-out among the millions of profiles that companies find in the site.

Of the other two solutions that LinkedIn provides, advertising sales is not of interest to you because they are for companies; while membership subscriptions require you to pay a fee in order to receive additional services – the paid services.

Let us now understand the concept of Talent Solutions that LinkedIn provides. While Talent Solutions are required by companies, you can take advantage of the concept of the solutions that LinkedIn provides member companies. This will help you to tailor make your profile to suit the requirements of the companies you want to target.

The most visible talent solution that LinkedIn provides recruiters is the LinkedIn Recruiter. LinkedIn Recruiter allows recruiters to get unlimited access to the best talent on LinkedIn. It is a one-stop solution for companies and recruiters to find, engage, and nurture ideal candidates faster and more cost-effectively than ever before. (https://business.linkedin.com/content/dam/business/talent-solutions/global/en_US/site/pdf/datasheets/linkedin-recruiter-datasheet-en-us.pdf)

You may be wondering why you should understand about LinkedIn Recruiter. One thing I have learnt over so many years of experience is this, "Always Begin with the End in Mind."

When you know where you want to go, you can then take the right steps today, so that you can reach your goal. So, an understanding of what recruiters and companies look for can help you immensely.

Let us now understand what LinkedIn Recruiter does for companies and recruiters. I have also recommended your line of action below each advantage.

LinkedIn Recruiter allows recruiters to get unlimited access to anyone on LinkedIn
Recruiters can expand their reach far beyond their personal network and search from the widest and most qualified talent pool of over 332+ million members.

What does this mean for you? It means that you are among the 332+ million members that companies can search seamlessly. You may be in the personal network of a few recruiters, but there are many others out there you do not know and they are all waiting to get a pie of you, searching for people like you, day-in and day-out.

LinkedIn Recruiter allows recruiters to find the best talent faster with targeted search filters
Recruiters can create more than 20 filters to help them breeze through even the toughest searches for candidates on LinkedIn. LinkedIn Recruiter provides the most advanced search interfaces and exclusive refinement filters, including years spent at a company, and field of study. This makes it easy for recruiters to find talent.

What does this mean for you? It indicates that recruiters can create filters to search the best talent on LinkedIn, and the number of filters that a recruiter can create is more than 20. This is an indication that there is a lot of competition out there on LinkedIn and you need to be at your best. You need to ensure that you are among the top five percentile of resumes that pop up when a recruiter searches for talent similar to what you have.

LinkedIn Recruiter allows recruiters to contact candidates directly
Every recruiter gets 150 InMails per month to contact their most preferred candidates. Unused InMails roll over to the next month.

What does this mean for you? You need to be among the most preferred candidates of the recruiters you need to be in touch with. For e.g. if you are an MR in a pharma company, you need to be in the most preferred candidate list of all recruiters from Pharma companies, including your own company. Your company should fear that you may leave them any moment, and that will be a loss to their company, and are forced to take steps to ensure that you do not leave them.

LinkedIn Recruiter allows recruiters to boost their recruitment productivity

Recruiters can create up to 50 search alerts that help them to spot talent automatically. Recruiters can use One-to-Many InMail messages and saved templates to let them contact more candidates faster.

What does this mean for you? You want to be among those candidates that recruiters want to reach faster and spot your talent automatically, with the search alerts that they create.

LinkedIn Recruiter allows recruiters to stay on top of candidates
With the click of a button, recruiters can stay up-to-date on the activities of sought after candidates so that they are ready to reach out when the candidates are ready for a job change.

What does this mean for you? As a candidate, you want to keep yourself up-to-date on your profile and let them know when you are seeking a change. Recruiters would get to know about your recent activities, and give them an indication that you are ready for a change, allowing them to contact you and give your candidature preference over others.

There are some other advantages that LinkedIn Recruiter provides recruiters, but this is out of the purview as far as you, a candidate for the recruiters, are concerned. This includes analytical tools and keeping all recruiters on the same page, ensuring continuity of work, even if an old recruiter is replaced with a new recruiter, and others.

From the preceding sections, I believe that you have the power of ensuring that recruiters see you more often than others, and are particularly interested in you, contact you frequently, and that you are visible to them at various quarters within the LinkedIn network.

You are now ready to proceed next to understand what you should do to be in the limelight, having learnt that LinkedIn is a very effective tool to get recruited.

You need to search for jobs, but before you search for jobs, you need to create a profile and a brand around yourself, so that recruiters are able to see you frequently.

What I am going to present in the next few chapters of the book will help you immensely, irrespective of whether you have an account with LinkedIn or not. If you already have an account with LinkedIn, you can compare and determine if your profile is among the best; and if you do not have an account, then you can create one, ensuring that the recommendations presented below are adhered to.

Chapter 4 – Creating a Professional Resume

Now that you know LinkedIn provides you a very strong platform to showcase your talent, ability, and thought leadership, you need to start figuring out how to be among the few individuals in your field of expertise that companies would want to be regularly in touch with.

Remember, the better and stronger your profile is, the more are your chances of being heard and followed, and you will be able to create "Your Brand."

Your first step towards creating your brand is to create your profile on LinkedIn. But before you create your profile on LinkedIn, it is important that you create a professional resume. Your LinkedIn Profile is a reflection of your professional resume. I am not dwelling deep into the development of a professional resume.

Remember, your resume is the first piece of document that a recruiter reads, and he/she has only a few seconds to glance at the resume. If you (in the sense, your resume) is able to grasp the recruiter's attention, you have the upper hand.

You are tech savvy and know how to create profiles on LinkedIn. The resume that you prepare will give you an indication of what to include in your profile. After all, your LinkedIn profile is your online resume. The profile must be your "Copyright" in the sense that it should be so unique that no one should be able to copy any content from your resume.

"Everything you've wanted is on the other side of fear" – George Addair

Create a Very Basic Account

The best way to start creating your brand is to first create a very basic profile. The basic profile has only that information that is necessary for you to create the account on LinkedIn. I am assuming here that you do not have an account with LinkedIn as yet. For those who have an account, you can skip this.

Chapter 5 – Features of a LinkedIn Profile

After you create your basic account with LinkedIn, it is time for you to understand the features of LinkedIn that you should be aware of. Whether you currently have an account or newly created an account, understanding the features of LinkedIn Profile will be of help to you.

Features

Once you have your basic account in place, you are now ready to enhance your profile. I will give you a corollary here. If you are constructing a house, first the structure of the house is set up, next the walls are erected and painted, and then the tiles are laid and polished for completing the house.

Your profile is like the house I described above. When you create your basic account, you only have the basic structure ready. Once this is done, you will now move to developing your profile, adding details that will make it stand out.

In this chapter, I have presented only the features of a LinkedIn Profile. In the subsequent chapters, I will explain what each of these mean, and how you can your profile stand out.

Name: Your name is your name. Keep it as it is.

Your Headline: This information, by default, presents your current job title.

"The only way to do great work is to love what you do" – Steve Jobs

Your location: Your location is where you are currently located. It is generally the place where you are currently working.

Your industry: Your industry is the industrial sector in which you are currently employed.

Photo: You should include your photo here. I will explain what kind of photograph should be used in subsequent chapters.

Contact Info: Your contact information, including your address and phone numbers are presented here.

Summary: Summary includes your mission, objectives and an overview of what you are. It is important that you keep updating this, based on your changed positions, your career aspirations and goals. In the subsequent chapter, I will describe what makes a good summary.

Experience: Your work experience is put in here. The experience is saved in reverse chronological order and you can indicate the company you are working for, your designation, duration, roles and responsibilities. You can also include experience in the military, volunteering, pro-sports, etc. I will explain how to record your experience in the experience section.

Education: Include all education and school information. You are aware of the courses you have studied and the school from where you have graduated, so I am not going to elaborate on this topic further.

Recommendations: Recommendations work like references. Unlike references, you can always ask for a recommendation from your network anytime. In references, you seek reference only when you are actively focusing on completing the negotiation with a company.

Certifications: Any certifications and licenses that you hold are to be included here. I will explain how to fill in this section in the next chapter.

Courses: This is in addition to the educational qualifications that you have. You can include courses on computers that you may have taken up in your school / college or university level.

Honors and Awards: All honors and awards you have received, academic as well as co-curricular, like sports, arts and crafts, etc.

Languages: You can show off all your language skills here – read, write and speak.

Organizations: You can list all organizations you are a member with. I will elaborate on this in the next chapter.

Patents: You can include any patents, copyrights and trademarks that you may have applied for during your work. A detailed explanation will be seen in the next chapter.

Publications: Some of you may have interest in writing books, research papers and articles. You can include these in the publication section.

Projects: Projects showcase your talent on handling people, logistics and your overall managerial skills. You can showcase these skills in the Projects section.

Skills and Endorsements: Skills and Endorsements indicate what your colleagues and people in your network think you are good at. The larger the number of endorsements for a particular skill, the better you are at that particular skill. This will help recruiters to find you quickly when the search for a skill that you have.

Test Scores: You can add test scores of various tests that you may have taken up in the past. It could be IELTS, TOEFL, GMAT, GRE, or any other test that you have taken, including certification tests.

Volunteer Experience and Causes: A number of companies seek individuals who are deeply associated with a cause. You can volunteer for a cause, and earn valuable experience because you are deeply involved in something. This involvement will also translate to an involvement in the organization of your choice, and organizations value your ability to not only to contribute to the organization but also to society at large.

Additional Information: Includes your birthday, hobbies and interests, marital status, and advice for people to contact you.

Chapter 6 – Sections That Focus on Who You Are

In the previous chapter you were exposed to the features of a LinkedIn profile. In this chapter, I will explain those features of the profile that focus on you, as an individual. The remaining features of the profile should focus on how you can help others, specifically the companies you are targeting to get hired. This will help you balance your profile.

Recalling the features from the previous chapter, you can easily figure out that those features of the profile that focus on you, and this includes:

1. Name and Photograph
2. Address, Contact Details and Location
3. Your email ID
4. Date of Birth
5. Hobbies and interests and languages
6. Your Educational Qualifications and Certificates
7. Your industry
8. Tests, Honors, Awards and Academic Achievements

Your name and Photograph – you never change your name every year or every two years! Probably one of the very few information that remains static in your profile. You have only your photograph right, not someone else's photograph!

"I hire people better than me and then get out of their way" – Lee Iacocca

Your date of birth – you can never change the day you were born. Another complete static information in your profile. This reminds me of a joke. A lady asked a young boy what his age was. He said he was 9 years old. The lady replied that he had been telling this for the past four years. The boy retorted back saying, "I am not among those who tell one thing one day and something else on another day!☺

Your email ID – keep it constant, because you would want to have only one email ID for all your transactions on LinkedIn. Ideally, LinkedIn would prefer you to include your professional email ID. While your professional email ID may change, if you change your organization, you can have one personal Email ID to keep track of your network. If you are using a personal Id, make sure that the id has a professional tone to it. Avoid using fancy personal email Ids. A student of someone I know had an email id cutegirl03@gmail.com. Such email ids convey a nonchalant and casual attitude.

Hobbies, Interests, Languages that you know are generally constant after you attain a certain age, and as a working professional, you would want to have only a handful of hobbies and interests, including knowing some foreign languages. To that extent, you can keep this static. However, some of you may be interested in learning something new. So, I am not discounting this, and you can always get back to update this information. Do not list too many hobbies and interest. The key here is not about quantity, but about quality. If you have interest in Tennis, and your favourite player is FedEx, then get to know more about FedEx, the number of Grand Slam titles he has won, his overall number of titles, career prize money, the country he belongs to, in short everything related to FedEx.

There are some who know a number of languages, while others know only one or two. It really does not matter as to how many languages you know, as long as you are able to convince someone that you really know the language, and are able to converse easily with someone native to the language.

Your Education Qualifications and Certificates: Unless you are an academician, and would want to take up additional educational qualifications, your educational qualification remains static after you have completed your graduation / post-graduation. As a working professional, you may be interested in taking up additional certificate courses to enhance your employability in the firm or industry. This feature is quite dynamic based on your interest levels. Never fake your educational qualifications and certificates on LinkedIn. You will end up losing not only your account with LinkedIn but also face criminal lawsuit against you. Make sure you include the year in which you completed the certificate course and the grade you achieved in your course.

Your Industry: Your industry will remain the same since you joined, because each industry has its unique features and if you are working in one particular industry, it will be difficult for you to change the industry. If you are an HR professional in a software company, your industry will be software and BPO, and you will find difficulty in moving into a factory set up, because your focus is on knowledge workers, not on factory workers. So, your experience is unique to the industry.

Tests, Honors, Awards and Academic Achievements: Add all your achievements, test scores and honors you received during your lifetime here. And why shouldn't you add? This is what makes you unique, stand out among the crowd for what you are. Gold Medals in Academics, Sports, Music, and other extra and co-curricular activities are valued by many companies, and give recruiters an idea of your all-round ability.

The information presented here is yours, nobody can take it away from you – your educational qualifications, your hobbies, interests and the languages you know, the certificates that you have attained through your hard work, are unique to you. You ought to be PROUD of what you have achieved, of being an alumni of a reputed educational institution, and your academic achievements and the knowledge that you have gained with your education.

Be proud about what and who you are, and this should reflect in your profile. But this is not the end of your profile. Every individual has something special in him or her, that has led them to be where they are today; and everyone loves to be given importance.

Do you remember, before creating your LinkedIn profile, I had recommended you to prepare an excellent professional resume? This is where the resume comes in handy. Make sure that you capture the essence of your resume into these sections of your LinkedIn Profile.

Chapter 7 – Sections that Focus on What You Can Do

In addition to the sections in your LinkedIn Profile that focus on who you are, there are sections that focus on what you can do. This is where you need to be very careful. Any focus on what you are will lead to loss of your credibility and recruiters may not be interested in your profile. You may be branded as someone who has a self-serving bias and would not consider initiating a discussion with you.

Let us check out these sections and understand what need to go into them.

The sections that would appear here would include

1. Your headline
2. Summary
3. Experience
4. Recommendations
5. Skills and Endorsements
6. Organizations
7. Patents
8. Publications
9. Volunteer Experience and Causes
10. Any Additional Information

> *"Human resources isn't a thing we do; it's the thing that runs our business"* – Steve Wynn

Any recruiter or company would actually be interested to know more about what you can do for their company, and the above sections would be more critical as compared to the sections presented in the previous chapter.

Everyone likes to brag what he or she is, but very few take the courage to let others know what they can do. While the points in the previous paragraph are good, they are not good enough to get you a job.

The difference between getting a job and not lies in how you can present your information on these sections.

Your personal brand on LinkedIn is completely dependent on how active you ae within your network. To remain active, you need to update your profile with what you do, your achievements, and your comments on your colleagues' promotions, endorsing your colleagues and co-workers, and sharing your contents on thought leadership.

Chapter 8 – Your Headline and Summary

If you have a resume, the first thing that any recruiter would notice is your headline and summary. If you are not able to convince a recruiter with your headline and summary, you can be rest assured that the recruiter has trashed your resume.

The same universal truth holds here too.

Your Headline is a one-line statement that identifies what you can do for the company. It is equivalent to the objective of your resume, though the objective is elaborate and covers what you are currently doing and what you would want to do in future.

Consider these headlines of two individuals, Nicholas and Francis, and figure out which is better.

    a.   Nicholas - Experienced Management professional
    b.   Francis - Experienced management professional, serial entrepreneur, investor, mentor and educator

Obviously, in this case, you would choose headline b, because it conveys not only more information, but you can also make out that the person has achieved a lot, wants to give back to society.

> *"Great vision without great people is irrelevant"- Jim Collins*

The first option tells you that the individual is a seasoned management professional, but you have no idea in which field of management, and how he will be helpful to your organization.

As a recruiter, wanting to recruit a seasoned individual for a board position to oversee strategy, you would prefer someone who can mentor, get in investments and educate people, and the moment you lay your eyes on this headline, you would want to know more about him.

Think over twice, thrice, four or five times or may be more, but keep revising your headline till you are able to arrive at the one headline that conveys what you can do for the company you want to join.

Now, let me shift my focus to the summary of your profile.

Your summary gives a snapshot of what you are and what you can do for the company.

Let me take the previous example again here.

Summary of Nicholas:
1. Over 20 years' experience in Marketing FMCG products
2. Well versed in managing distribution channels and handling stockists and Carrying and Forwarding Agents
3. Was the master negotiator for the company

Summary of Francis:
1. Over 20 years of experience in Marketing FMCG products and Over the shelf Software products
2. Set up 3 software companies in the telecom, educational and ERP products space, continuing to be the Chairman of these companies
3. Passionate mentor and entrepreneurship educator, having mentored 10 companies in the past 5 years and planning to mentor 20 more in the next 5 years
4. Keen to invest on ventures in the software product space, focusing on cutting edge technology for driverless cars, energy efficient public transport systems, renewable energy solutions and energy efficient lighting systems

As a recruiter of a company that manufactures LED Bulbs, who would you consider among the two?

I know you would choose the second one. Why? Is it because he has included four points, as compared to three of the first individual?

While you think of a good answer for considering the second individual as the right fit, let me explain how to write an excellent summary.

Whenever you write a summary, you need to consider the following points.

Analyze who your audience is, because your summary is written for them

When you analyze who your audience is, you need to consider answering the following questions.

a. What do you want them to know about you?
b. What do you want them to do?
c. How do you want them to feel?

Once you have figured out what your audience requires, it is time for you to get to the second stage where you prepare the raw content.

Prepare your raw content

Your raw content should cover the following six aspects of your summary.

a. Victories or accomplishments – a line or two about your significant achievements. E.g. achieved a significant reduction in operational cost; increased revenue for 3 years in a row for the X product range by

b. Values and Passions – A list of areas that inspire and energize you, pushing you to do your best. It could be something as simple as creativity to becoming members of complex societies and organizations

c. Valiant Superpowers – enlist skills that others do not have and make you a really special person in your team. E.g. you are a fun person to be with, make the office lively and there is never a dull moment when you are around.

d. Vital Statistics – any vital statistics that significantly highlights your profile. E.g. reduced cost by $50 million for the organization by taking A, B and C measures
e. Verve – anything quirky about you, differentiating you from your colleagues and peers. E.g. night owl, love to sing songs when meetings start getting boring
f. Validation – any accolades and awards bestowed upon you

You are now ready to write your summary
You can use the first person or the third person formats. Both are acceptable. When you use the first person, you are more likely to connect with the recruiter.

E.g. I started my first business in a long distance train when I showed a movie to the guests in the coach I was traveling in.

Read your summary aloud
Read your summary aloud, word by word, as if you were reading it to an audience for the first time and ask the following questions.
a. Does the first line want you to read the summary further?
b. Is the summary authentic?
c. Does it differentiate you from your peers?
d. Does your summary attract the attention of decision makers – read recruiters?
e. Have you provided interesting facts for the recruiter to know more about you?
f. Does it contain enough personal information about you; about 20-30%?
g. Does your summary explain how you are adding value to the decision maker?
h. Does your writing style convey your personality?
i. Have you formatted it beautifully, with enough blank spaces and power headlines to make it easier for someone to read?
j. Have you included external validation?
k. Is your summary grammatically correct and proofread?
l. Does your summary include all the keywords that you wanted to be featured in it?

m. Is your reader (read recruiter) interested to know more about you and take appropriate action?

Another way you can evaluate the effectiveness of the summary is to run it through a test audience. You can ask three of your friends, I mean, real friends, who genuinely care for your success, to help you out by giving an honest feedback. If you are not able to get them, even acquaintances would do, but make sure that they do not have any ulterior or self-serving motive in helping you out.

Run the summary through them and ask them the following questions.
   a. Is it an accurate representation of who you are?
   b. Do they want to learn more about you?
   c. Is there anything missing?
   d. What changes are required to improve it?

You can use either of these methods to figure out what you need to include, change and omit from your summary.

When you use the former method, you can rate your answers on a rating scale of $1 - 3$. So, you can have a cumulative minimum of 13 and a maximum of 39. If, after you have scored the questions and tallied the responses, your score is less than 29, then you need to seriously need to have a re-look on your summary and improve it.

You are now ready to bring your brand to life
You are now ready with your summary. You can include it in your LinkedIn Profile, to attract recruiters to read more about your profile when they search you on LinkedIn.

I had pointed out that when you write the summary, it should be free from all grammatical and spelling errors. However, in spite of all precautions that you may take, some bloopers may always occur. In such cases, if you have done a spell check using the Grammar and Spell Check functionality of MS Word, it may not be sufficient. It needs to be proofread, thoroughly.

Let me point out some really nasty and hilarious bloopers that can creep in when you write your summary.

1. I am very good at pubic relations (public, has become pubic)
2. Instrumental in ruining the operations of a Midwest chain store (running has become ruining)
3. Revolved customer problems and inquiries (resolved has become revolved)
4. Consistently tanked top sales producer for new accounts (ranked became tanked)
5. Demonstrated ability in multi-tasting (instead of multi-tasking)
6. I am fluent in English and Spinach (read Spanish)

Can you make out any spelling or grammatical errors in these bloopers? I don't really think so, because grammatically they are correct, and neither there are any spelling mistakes. So, it is all the more important that you run your summary through both the tests that I described above – the 13 questions test and the mock audience test. It will help you go a long way.

Your summary is your first step in establishing your personal brand as well as be in the limelight with recruiters of your choice.

You are required to do a lot more than prepare the summary and be done with it.

Let me come back to the first question I had asked you. Were you able to figure out whose summary is best and why?

I would want you to do this exercise on the two summaries. You obviously know the better of the two, but from a practice perspective, if you had written these summaries, how would you rate them, or what would your rating points be for each of these questions?

Last, but not least, do not consider these summaries as the final. There may be many ways in which you can improve them. As an exercise, I have compared two summaries, and provided them so that you can identify the one that is better. You may be able to find better descriptions to write, if you adhere to some of the principles mentioned in this chapter.

Chapter 9 – Experience

Your headline and summary are the stepping stones in your quest for finding a job through LinkedIn. However, your profile is never complete without your experience. Even if you do not have work experience, it is important that you showcase your internship experience here.

The experience section informs prospective employers and recruiters what you are capable of.

Let us start with an example. I will again use the example that I have cited in the previous chapter.

Experience Details of Nicholas: for sake of simplicity, I have included only the last employment details.

Organization: ABC, Inc.
Location: Guangzhou, China
From: Sep 2009 till date
Responsibilities:

    a. Handled the Hong Kong, Macau and Guangzhou regions of China
    b. Was responsible for the marketing of confectionery, bakery, home care, personal care and oral hygiene products
    c. Managed a distribution network of 50 distributors and 1000 retailers
    d. A team of 5 marketing managers, 20 sales managers, 2 marketing executives, 50 sales executives, 1 HR Manager, 2 HR executives, 1 Finance Manager and 1 accounts executive reported to me.

> *"One cannot hire a hand; a whole man always comes with it"- Peter Drucker*

Experience Details of Francis: for sake of simplicity, I have included only the last employment details.

Organization: XYZ Limited
From: Jun 2003 till date
Responsibilities

a. As President of XYZ Limited, invested a total of $15 million in three ventures – XYZ Software Solutions, EduSoft, Inc. and XYZ Telecom Solutions
b. Achieved a turnover of $4 million, $6 million and $3 million each in the year 2014
c. Received 6 patents, 2 for each business, and have filed for 12 more patents on specific software developed
d. Mentored 10 ventures and all ventures are generating million dollar revenues in various industries
e. Teach entrepreneurship at National University of Singapore, Nanyang Technological University, University of Waterloo, and University of Auckland, New Zealand

So, if you were a recruiter / hiring manager, and you had to hire one individual from among the two, who will you hire for the position of a board member in your organization?

Your answer is too obvious, Francis. I would again ask you the same question, why? Because Francis has included 5 points as compared to 4 by Nicholas? Or is there something unique about the way Francis has presented his experience details?

Before you answer these questions, let us take time to consider what makes an excellent description of experience.

Start with an overview
It is a good idea for you to provide an overview of what your job entails, like what you managed – budget, people, purchase, etc.

Use Action Words
Never use terms like responsible, handled, or duties included. No one is interested to know what your responsibilities were. Recruiters and

hiring managers are more interested to know what you achieved; what difference you made to the organization you worked for. To that extent, it is better for you to use action words, like achieved, reduced cost by x%, increased revenue by $Y million, etc.

Use frequently searched keywords

Use keywords specific to your skills and job descriptions, that are frequently used by recruiters and hiring managers. Using highly searched keywords ensures that you are always on the top in the recruiters' search criteria.

Be concise and clear

Veracity is the name of the game. Wherever possible, reduce the number of words. If you can use one word to explain something instead of four, why use four? You can use the space saved to write something you could never think of.

Use the correct tense

Use present tense for your current job responsibilities and past tense for previous job responsibilities.

Don't overuse the bullets

Some people think that it is great to write down all responsibilities as a series of bullets. Well, if you consider this the best, then think again. No one has time to read a long list of bulleted items. As far as possible, try to break the responsibilities in terms of an overview and achievements, leaving enough white space between.

Frontload your achievements

Instead of saying, "Was promoted to Sales Manager and achieved a 12% increase in sales," say, "Achieved a 12% increase in sales after I was promoted to a Sales Manager."

Always ensure that your achievement comes first, rest later. Remember the adage, "Always put the donkey last."

Check for Spelling and Grammar

One pet peeve for most recruiters is spelling and grammar. The moment you have typos in your profile, experience or anywhere, you are doomed, and recruiters and hiring managers would give your profile a cold shoulder.

Link to your company page

When you provide your experience with a company, and it has a company page on LinkedIn, make sure that you link your organization to the company page. This informs recruiters and hiring managers that you are currently employed with this firm.

Now, let us get back to the two descriptions given. Which of the two given descriptions meet the guidelines presented above.

No guesses for this one – Francis' description closely meets the criteria presented. I believe the description can still be improved.

Chapter 10 – Organizations and Volunteer Experience

Volunteer Experience
Whether you are joining a firm or a college or a university, experience always counts. But what if you have no experience what will you do? Will you be at an advantage if you have volunteered and interned in an organization? What if the organization was a not-for-profit organization which did not pay you for your volunteer service?

As an individual, would you value this experience? Or would you rather prefer to have only paid experience, as in working for a company or a firm?

If you were a recruiter, and you come across an individual's profile who spends 10 to 15 hours every week as a volunteer in a local church or school for special children. Would you consider hiring this individual in your organization?

If your answer for hiring such an individual is No, then probably you are losing out on hiring someone who can provide deep insights on providing sustainable solutions to societal problems.

I know that most of you would prefer to hire someone with volunteer experience, because he/she brings a number of advantages to your organization, in addition to providing sustainable solutions to societal problems.

Have you ever worked as a volunteer for Non Gazetted Organizations or for any local charity trust? If yes, then you are a very highly valued possession.

"Mind is everything. What you think you become"- Buddha

The advantages of getting someone with volunteer experience includes the following:

A. Gain New Experience and Insights

Volunteering, if done right, can help you develop new experience and deep insights into solving problems that society faces at large. Society can be your immediate neighborhood, your state, your nation or any international location.

I know individuals who travel across the world to work as a volunteer in an alien land, and learn to appreciate diversity. They acquire technical, social and academic skills that they cannot learn in a classroom environment. Volunteering helps people realize their latent talent, interests, hobbies and opinions. The fact that you are not paid for volunteer work requires a lot of motivation, internally and externally. Money, definitely is not a motivator, but the satisfaction of seeing someone happy, getting involved in the progress of society, helping underprivileged students study and make them respectable citizens of society will bring out an inner peace that you may have never felt before.

The important thing to remember here is that volunteering is not a numbers driven activity. If you boast of volunteering for 15 organizations in the last 5 years, it means that you have averaged about 3 per year, but have you contributed sufficiently to ensure the organization's success?

Rather than talking how many organizations you have volunteered in, why don't you write about what you have done there? Similar to how you record your experience, where you highlight your achievements?

Your achievements in volunteering is an indication of your future success in the rigorous corporate environment.

So, never hesitate to display your volunteer experience. It will help you go a long way in achieving success in every field of your life.

B. You learn to give back to society and help others

I am not sure how many of you have read the world's longest epic, The Mahabharata. I am particularly interested in the character of Karna, the unfortunate warrior. Born to a princess through a boon from the Sun God before her marriage, he was abandoned at birth. When Karna was born, he had a breastplate armor and ear-rings that made him invincible to any arrow or weapon.

Years later, before the Mahabharata war, Indra, the King of the Lords, visits Karna in disguise. Karna prayed to the Sun God, his father and donated wealth to the poor and needy at the end of his prayers. Indra visits Karna after he has completed his prayers and is getting ready to donate. Indra informs Karna that he wants his breastplate armor and ear-rings, and Karna happily donates them, knowing fully that by donating, he can be killed in the war.

The purpose of this story is not to eulogize the epic or donate something you are strong at. The purpose was to drive home the fact that there is a joy in giving. In the Mahabharata, Karna felt immensely satisfied in giving to the poor, and felt blissful after such noble deeds.

As a volunteer, you learn to give back to society. You are adept in creating sustainable environments for others, create healthier communities and brighten the lives of those around you.

C. Creating Connections with People

By volunteering, you understand the value of creating connections with people. You realize that in today's world, networking is very crucial, helping you develop various positive traits that employers will find useful. Volunteering helps you meet a wide variety of people from various walks of life, allowing you to widen your knowledge base.

D. You get a sense of Accomplishment

Trust me, those of you who have volunteered realize that volunteering is not a very sexy, glamorous, easy and plush job; however, you will find volunteering uplifting and highly beneficial. While you don't receive any monetary rewards, you live to share your experience with others, and the experience you gain carries more value than any monetary benefit you could possibly have earned.

Volunteering is doing your own work, taking time off from your daily schedules and helping others. It boosts your confidence, makes you feel good and lifts up your spirits.

E. Building Career Options

Volunteering helps you to test out your desired career path. You also get an edge on your resume. You get an opportunity to work for an organization that shares ideals and interests similar to yours is a great way to get going. This is particularly important if you are inexperienced and offers an opportunity to be part of a productive workforce from day one.

Volunteering may not give you money, as explained earlier, but gives you a sense of satisfaction, accomplishment, connections and a voice to be heard. Forget about being competitive and the urge to beat out competition. You get to be yourself, and that's the most important thing you can do to get your career going.

Highlighting your volunteering experience indicates that you love being yourself and that you are interested in developing sustainable solutions that help society at large. Volunteering experience also indicates to prospective employers that you have a strong network to back you up, and this network of references will help you in the long run.

Organizations
In addition to your volunteering experience, it also helps you to be associated with a professional organization. Many organizations provide assistance to their members on a professional front. For e.g. if you are a member of IEEE, you not only get to know the latest developments in the field of electrical and electronics engineering, but

also get access to a wide variety of tools that IEEE provides to its members, and you can use these tools in your professional life.

Such organizations also give you an opportunity to network with others in the industry, and your knowledge base widens, leading to a faster professional progress.

You need to pay to become a member of the organization, but it is worth paying because you get access to a wide variety of resources.

Chapter 11 – Recommendations, Skills and Endorsements

Recommendations, skills and endorsements indicate what you are good at, but you do not recommend yourself, nor do you endorse your own skills.

Recommendations and endorsements provide you opportunities to gather "social proof" of who and what you are. People in your network vouch for your skills and experience, allowing you to increase your credibility to prospective employers.

You may be pretty aware of the difference between recommendations and endorsements, so, I wouldn't want to spend much time on this topic. However, what is of interest is how to get more endorsements and better recommendations.

Endorsements indicate that you are excellent in a set of skills that people have seen you exhibit.

Recommendations, on the other hand, are more meaningful and provide an insight about you as an individual. People who have worked with you are willing to put their reputation at stake, to support you and your abilities. It indicates that people in your network trust you, and inform others that they can also trust you.

"Strive not to be a success, but rather to be of value"- Albert Einstein

Writing a recommendation takes time and effort, and that's why recommendations are very powerful tools for recruiting candidates from LinkedIn.

Endorsements

In this section, I will inform you about how to get more endorsements so that when your endorsed skills are searched, your name surfaces at the top.

A. Add your most relevant skill
If you believe that you need to have a very large number of skills because you need to show prospective employers the variety of skills you possess, then you need to think again.

A large number of skills would overwhelm people in your network to endorse you, and it may also be difficult for them to remember whether you are really good at any specific skill.

Start with a small number of skills that are very relevant to what you are currently doing. You can have about 4 – 6 skills that you are really good at, relevant and currently utilizing them.

A small number of skills would mean people in your network can easily recall them, and you can get more endorsements for these skills, as compared to having too many skills.

Remember, prospective employers and recruiters are attracted to profiles that have numerous endorsements for a few skills than less endorsements for a variety of skills.

B. Remove all irrelevant skills
These are skills that do not have an impact on your career. They are better removed than retained in your profile.

Think of this situation. You have indicated a skill that you are not too adept in using, and a number of people endorse you for the same. Your name surfaces at the top when a recruiter searches for this skill, and he thinks you really have this skill, and asks you to meet him. What will you do? You may not have the strength or confidence to face the recruiter, because you have not used this particular skill for a very long time now.

It is best to avoid such situations and stick to those skills that are relevant to what you are currently doing.

It is better to have 6 skills with 20 endorsements each, than have 20 skills with 6 endorsements each.

C. Move endorsements to the top of your profile

It has been observed that when you move endorsements to the top of your profile, you get more endorsements. When I say top of your profile, it is not at the very top, but below the summary. It is an ideal place to fit in your skills and endorsements because when a person visits your profile, he/she is tempted to endorse you for those skills.

D. Endorse others

One foolproof way to receive endorsements is by giving endorsements. The law of reciprocity plays here. Start endorsing your most recent colleagues. The more you endorse them, the more likely they are to return the favour.

When you endorse people you don't know, but have been following their updates, they would return the favour by endorsing you too.

E. Ask people to endorse you

You can ask people to endorse you for the skills you possess. You can get in touch with your ex-coworkers and colleagues, request them to endorse you.

You, in turn, need to endorse them, or should have endorsed them in the past, so that the law of reciprocity is maintained.

F. Get people to your LinkedIn Profile

You can link your LinkedIn account with your other social networking accounts, so that your LinkedIn Updates get to reach a maximum number of audience.

G. Include a request to endorse you in your summary

Whenever someone visits your profile on LinkedIn, they may or may not endorse you, but you can always leave a message for visitors to endorse you for your skills.

H. You can offer an incentive to anyone who endorses you

This is a risky proposition and you will have to be very careful if you want to adopt this method. You may want to offer an e-book to anyone who endorses you or a small gift that would be delivered to their address.

I. Update your status often

Keep updating your status once a week. Anything more than once or twice a week would mean no one would be interested in following your updates.

Once a week updates would lead to more people viewing your profile, and endorsing you for your skills.

J. Finally, never forget to say Thanks

A very simple Thank You Note can do wonders for people who endorse you.

"Thanks ... for endorsing me... I really appreciate the time you have taken to endorse me for my skills... If you need any assistance in your business or otherwise, you are free to contact me."

You follow these steps and can get endorsements. The best way, however, is to give endorsements to as many people as you want and it will return back to you with interest.

So much for endorsements.

While endorsements indicate what you are good at, you also need recommendations that give you the edge over your competitors.

Recommendations

You cannot write your own recommendations nor can you edit the recommendation someone has written for you. However, your recommendations are visible to the entire LinkedIn Community, and this is the reason why recommendations carry a lot of weight, as compared to endorsements in the community.

Through recommendations, a third party, can get a better perspective about you and your business expertise and abilities.

1. To a potential employer, a LinkedIn recommendation is a reference in advance.
2. To a potential customer, a LinkedIn recommendation is a proof to base a purchase decision on.

Recommendations are miniature reference letters that you write in favour of your coworkers, employees, employers, customers, suppliers and colleagues. You vouch for someone through these recommendations, rather than "Like" someone on Facebook.

If you plan to get a recommendation, you need to give recommendations. What I am presenting below is to help you write excellent recommendations so that you can get similar recommendations from others.

Giving Recommendations

A. Be Specific
Whenever you need to recommend someone, be very specific to highlight what the person has demonstrated. Your language should reflect the abilities and skills that the person exhibits.

Make sure that you highlight skills that are transferrable from one job to another, what they do best, and why they are different. People expect to see positive comments and anything specific about them is always welcome.

It is not sufficient for you to say someone is "Outstanding," because it does not give any insight into the abilities of the person about whom you are giving recommendation.

Make sure that the person is really "Outstanding" in the field that you want to recommend him for.

B. Use Descriptive Words

User words that describe the individual. Be liberal in the use of adjectives, but not so liberal that you end up writing everything rosy about the individual. Use adjectives that are powerful and valuable, specific, interesting and somewhat unusual. Examples can be brilliant, vivacious, hardworking, honest, amazing, etc.

C. Be Memorable

When you need to make memorable recommendations, remember the Rule of Threes. The Rule of Threes states that if you write recommendations in groups of three, it is very easily registered, more interesting, enjoyable and memorable, satisfying, effective and useful.

The best part of the Rule of Threes is that it is simple, powerful and it works!

Consider this example:

"Ronald is an excellent HR professional with years of experience in HRM. He successfully manages a team of 50 HR professionals, HR Quality Circle, and an amazing mimicry artist. He is fun to work with, has an infectious smile and takes genuine interest in the welfare of people. He is the gatekeeper of the culture of his organization. If you need to hire someone who can change your organizational culture, Ronald is "The" one for you."

Compare this with the example below:

"Ronald is a seasoned HR professional, and I really enjoy working with him. You should hire Ronald for what he is."

If you compare the two recommendations, you can find that the second recommendation has nothing specific describing about the individual. The kind of feedback you give to your colleagues or others will reflect on the recommendations you will receive.

Having understood how to give recommendations, let us now shift our focus on how to seek recommendations.

Seeking Recommendations

Seeking a recommendation from a colleague, co-worker, customer, supplier or peer may seem awkward at first. But it is important that you learn the art of seeking recommendations, so that you can maximize the chances of people writing you a quality recommendation.

The following points will help you in acquiring the art of seeking recommendations.

A. Seek recommendations only from people you know or have worked with

This is the first and foremost rule that you need to remember when you seek a recommendation. Seeking a recommendation from someone you know is always better, because the person knows you very well, and is able give you an objective recommendation, following the rules that we discussed above.

B. Use the recommendation system that LinkedIn provides

Use the system that LinkedIn provides. When someone recommends you, it reflects back on the person who recommended you. You may find it awkward, but it is perfectly acceptable to request a recommendation email to your contact through the LinkedIn System. Make sure that the person who is giving the recommendation knows that his recommendation will be displayed on his LinkedIn Profile.

C. Request what you want

Have you ever written a recommendation to any of your contacts when he/she has requested you to provide a specific format for the recommendation?

How much easier would it be if someone told you what they wanted? For a job, or for getting venture capital for their new business?

Knowing the end result always makes it easier for one to provide a recommendation. Similarly, to make life easier for your contact, you can request what you want from your contact. Your contact will be more than happy to give you a recommendation because it is easy.

A recommendation request in the format below can be a useful place to start with:

"Hi Bill,

I am trying to complete my profile on LinkedIn to improve my professional credibility. I would like to thank you in advance for your willingness to write a recommendation for me. We have worked together on the condominium project about six months ago and I am sure you will be able to highlight my abilities, experience, statistical knowledge, ability to take on additional responsibilities, and project management capabilities.

I am using my LinkedIn Profile to help me become an expert in Project Management. If you feel comfortable recommending me for a new position in a large construction company, feel free to write about my credentials as mentioned above.

<Your Name>"

I am not guaranteeing you that will receive a recommendation, but a mail like this will force your contact to consider giving you a recommendation.

While it is important that you seek recommendation, you need to be aware of the timing of seeking the recommendation.

When to seek recommendation

Timing for seeking a recommendation becomes important because this will determine the appropriateness of the recommendation.

A. Anytime is a good time
For most recommendations, anytime is a good time to seek one. All you need to do is drop a mail through the LinkedIn system, specifying why you are seeking a recommendation and you will be obliged; provided you are equally adept in giving your recommendation to your contact.

B. After an amazing job
One of the best times to seek a recommendation is when you have achieved something, outstanding result, a promotion, or a salary raise. You can request your contact to recommend you for what you have achieved.

C. After a compliment
When someone compliments you for a favour you have done them, it is a good time to ask for a recommendation.

"Hi, thanks for your wonderful words, complimenting me for the work done well. Would you mind if you can give me a recommendation on my LinkedIn Profile? It will be very helpful."

To cut the long story short, you can get recommendations only if you start recommending others. The bottom line is to be active on LinkedIn, and start recommending others. You will get recommendations from them pretty soon.

Chapter 12 – Do's and Don'ts of a LinkedIn Profile

Let me now bring your attention to one of the most important aspects of your profile, the do's and don'ts. It is important that you focus follow these do's and don'ts so that you create a profile that is effective and conveys meaning to people in your network as well as to recruiters.

Let me explain the Do's first and then the Don'ts.

The Critical Do's

Personalize connection Requests
Whenever you want to send a connection request to someone you know make sure you write a personal message to the connection. If you send a message to someone you don't know, they are likely to hit the "Do Not Know" or "Report Spam" button. And you will lose the ability to send connection requests and you may have your account blocked for a few days.

Have a profile picture
It is important for you to have a profile picture, as it indicates that you have a professional outlook. The photograph should be professional, and you must be looking directly into the camera. A smiling, clean shaven face, well dressed would make a huge difference and recruiters and others would like to connect with you.

Personalize Recommendation Requests
Recommendations are like references. Whenever you request someone to give you a recommendation, please make a personalized request to the person you want the recommendation from. By giving a personal note, you are putting things in perspective, and you will also have no issue in reciprocating when the other person requests you a recommendation.

"Hire character, train skill"- Peter Schultz

Keep it Professional at all Times

It is important that you keep all your communication and posts professional. LinkedIn is a business social network, and everybody in the network does want everything to be professional and business oriented on the network.

Turn Off Notifications when Updating Your Profile

If you need to make too many updates on one single day, make sure you turn off notifications to your network. It is advisable that you turn off notifications, so that when people in your network see their profiles, they are not overburdened with too many notifications from you.

Send a Welcome Message that Provides Value

Whenever you have a new connect, it is a good practice to send a welcome message that provides the other person value. When you add a welcome message, the odds of getting a response are increased.

Regularly Nurture Relationships

It is important that you nurture relationships. These relationships are the ones that will help you in the long run. It can be a very simple thing as leaving a small positive comment to a posting or a Birthday wish, sending content that is useful for their profession, or even a message congratulating them on their new post or job or promotion. "Success comes through selflessness."

Make your contact list open to your connections

Never hide your contact lists to new connections. It is seen as a self-serving mechanism with an ulterior motive. If you send a connection request to someone, and he or she hides his or her connection list, how would you feel? Will you like it?

Introduce your connections to each other

If you need good referrals and recommendations, you need to be proactive with your business matchmaking, and the best you can do is to connect your connections if you feel there could be synergies.

Respond promptly to messages

Always treat LinkedIn messages as regular emails. 1-2 days for a response is perfectly fine, but anything beyond this is a complete no-no, and your connection loses interest in you.

The Critical Don'ts

Don't send spams

Never post messages that are self-serving, and can be relegated to spam. Always think about the others rather than you, when you have to send messages.

Don't over post

Avoid posting more than 2 messages a day. Twice or thrice a week is fine. This would irritate your connections because their emails get clogged with your update messages every half an hour or so.

Don't criticize negatively in comments or groups

I had already pointed out this issue earlier. However, I believe it is important that you read it again here. LinkedIn is a platform for making positive connections, not for negativity. And don't be that guy or girl, who becomes infamous for negative comments.

Do not post self-serving contents in groups

LinkedIn is not for spamming with your self-serving content. Whenever you want to share something, craft it so that it becomes useful to your group. It should add value to your group, otherwise it is better not posting it at all.

Don't send to messages to multiple people without unselecting this option

If you are sending a message to multiple people, unselect the button "Allow recipients to see each other's names and email addresses." Nobody likes a casually sent message to a bunch of people.

Don't ask people to like your Facebook page

One of the biggest mistakes many people make is to ask connections to like their Facebook Page. It is really, really lame. If you have a personal relationship with someone, and you are requesting him or her to like your Facebook page, it is a different ball game, but otherwise, don't indulge in such postings.

Don't ask new connections or people you don't know to endorse you

Never request people you don't know to endorse you. You may find a number of random people requesting them to endorse you. But my sincere request is to avoid giving these recommendations, because if they give you, you would be obliged to give a recommendation too, and if you do not know each other personally, then imagine the embarrassing situation you may put yourself in when someone requests you to personally vouch for the person in question.

Don't send a message, "You viewed my profile..."

You seem to be accusing the other person of snooping on your LinkedIn profile. If you really need to send a message, send a personalized message, but not one starting with, "I know you viewed my profile."

Don't treat LinkedIn like Facebook or Twitter

LinkedIn is very different from Facebook or Twitter. You can post any tweet or Facebook post regarding anything, like what you had for lunch, what you are wearing today, the perfume you used, and what not. LinkedIn is not a forum for these posts. So, it is best for you to keep things professional as far as LinkedIn is concerned.

Remember, recruiters can see all your posts, comments, recommendations and endorsements. When recruiters see such posts, they realize that you are not serious about your connections and give recommendations and endorsements without any thought about who the person is. This will definitely be seen negatively by recruiters, and you will not get an opportunity to impress recruiters.

Chapter 13 – Searching Jobs using LinkedIn

Having created a profile that you want to showcase on LinkedIn; you have even taken care to be sure that you get the right endorsements, are connected to the right people in your network and you are highlighted at the right places at the right time.

You are now looking for a job. Like most job portals, the LinkedIn job portal works in a very similar way. You need to remember the keywords that will get you to the company / companies that you are targeting.

For e.g. you can use keywords like Internet based Marketing, E-Marketing, web-marketing, SEO, SMM and SEM to search for job postings related to Internet Marketing.

Since companies are already part of the LinkedIn professional group, you can directly see the job postings of the companies that are already listed there. You can also search a job based on location, or search for positions or companies or use keywords to get to what you are looking for.

You can also check for jobs you have applied, searches and jobs that you have saved.

This is the basic search capability that you can find on LinkedIn.

You can also perform advanced searches on the job postings and search for companies seeking to hire your skillsets. You can search based on location, role, skills, level, and many more.

"The key for us, number one, has always been hiring very smart people"- Bill Gates

You can then apply to the job posting through LinkedIn or on their website.

Make sure that you read the job description thoroughly and understand what they are looking for. Unlike most job portals that I have seen and used, I find job postings on LinkedIn having a very detailed job description, as well as instructions on what needs to be done.

In addition to searching and applying for jobs, what is more interesting that you can do is to follow companies. The next chapter outlines what it means to follow companies and get updates.

Chapter 14 – Group Membership & Following Companies

In the previous chapter, you were introduced to the concept of job search on LinkedIn, and that you can search jobs based on location, position, and keywords.

However, the more interesting part is your ability to follow companies and get to know about their job postings, and all information related to what the company is doing.

From the figure, you can see that there are updates from various companies about what they intend to do, and you can keep a track of what is happening. They may even post a note stating that they are hiring for a particular position and are soliciting applications. You can apply to these companies directly with your LinkedIn profile.

In addition, if you are interested in following some companies, you can click on following, and you will get information that you are seeking about these companies.

So, you see, you can follow companies for what they do, their job postings, and other information that they post on LinkedIn.

You can like them, comment on them, and share the post on your page.

Doing so, will help recruiters understand that you like to follow their company, are keeping yourself updated about the developments of the company and are genuinely interested in the affairs of the

"Big jobs usually go to the men who prove their ability to outgrow small ones"- Ralph Waldo

company. You are also providing appropriate advice for the development of the company as well as suggesting innovative solutions for the company to implement.

Recruiters view this positively, and you are seen favorably among the recruiters, and you can boost your chances of being recruited by the company. This will also help you when you are called for an interview with the company officials. You will have less research to do and will know what the company requires and what you will be able to do for them

In addition to following companies, LinkedIn provides an added functionality of becoming members of groups. Groups in LinkedIn is when members with similar interests form a virtual group and share their ideas, documents, videos and other information using the LinkedIn platform. Members can contribute to the group activity by commenting, sharing data, and starting group discussions on LinkedIn.

Once you become a member of a group or some groups, it is important for you to contribute to the group activity.

Think of it this way. If you were to start a group and you find that none of the group members have time to contribute to the development of the group, be it in terms of intellectual or otherwise, then how would you feel?

It is in this perspective that you need to contribute to group activity. When you contribute to group activity, you share any of the following:
1. Your comments to a post by a group member
2. Post a document that you think is relevant for people to read and enjoy
3. Initiate a discussion on any topic within a group
4. Finally, create your own group
5. In addition to these above ways of contributing to a group activity, you can also do your bit by ensuring that the content posted is not offensive to anyone. In a professional forum, offend a group of people is never accepted and leaves a bad taste in the mouth. If you find any such posting, you can help by indicating that such posts be removed.

For you to create your personal brand and be visible in various forums, it is important that you contribute regularly to your groups' activities.

Make sure that you limit your discussions to the professional front. Anything personal will always be taken negatively, and your comments may be deleted or you may be removed from the group's functioning because you have not adhered to the basic rules regulating the operation of groups on LinkedIn.

Chapter 15 – Companies and Groups: Differences

Before I move on to highlighting some important tips for effective job search, I would like to indicate the differences between companies and groups as you see in LinkedIn.

Sl. No.	Companies	Groups
1	Have a company page	Have a group page
2	You cannot become a member of the company page	You can become a member of the group page
3	You can follow updates and write comments	You can follow updates, write comments and contribute positively towards group development
4	You are connected to the company authorized representative for access to information	You have many connections and you can share ideas with them. Your connections can also include employees from the companies you are seeking employment from
5	Companies can post job openings in LinkedIn	Groups cannot post job openings, but companies can post job openings in these groups

I believe these are the 5 major differences that you can figure out if you review the Groups and Companies sections in LinkedIn.

"Winning isn't everything but WANTING to Win is"- Vince Lombardi

Chapter 16 – Thought Leadership

There are two prominent ways in which you can contribute to thought leadership in LinkedIn.

Of course, you do have the comments that you share and the post that you make as part of your group activities, but I believe that it is necessary for you to know that there are other ways you can contribute to though leadership.

The first way is through using SlideShare and the second way is by using LinkedIn Pulse. Let us check how these can contribute to enhancing your personal brand.

SlideShare (www.slideshare.net)

SlideShare was started with a simple goal of sharing knowledge online. Today, SlideShare is the world's largest community for sharing presentations and other professional content.

SlideShare was founded in Oct 2006 and was acquired by LinkedIn in May 2012.

As a user, SlideShare allows you to easily upload and share presentations, infographics, documents, videos, and webinars.

What is the benefit for you?

You can view more than 15 million uploads from individuals and organizations on a wide range of topics, like technology and business to travel, health, education and many more. You can also search and find what interests you, learn from top contributors like Guy Kawasaki, The White House, Mashable and many more.

"Time spent on hiring is time well spent"- Robert Half

You may also find your neighbor or the guy/girl sitting next to you is a top contributor, and you can learn from them.

But why should you only learn from what your friends, colleagues and others in your network put up? Why can't you put up what you have learnt, and share them with the rest of the world? Wouldn't that be great?

You can see from the three presentations in the screenshot that they have different number of views. One has 3973 views, while the second has 1399 and the third has 1147 views. Obviously, if you were a recruiter, you would prefer the one with the highest number of views, because there if there are so many people downloading or viewing one presentation, the presentation must have some substance.

As a candidate, you would want to highlight and showcase your talent and expertise in your field, and SlideShare is an excellent platform for you to showcase your talent. The more the number of slides you upload, the more the number of people would get to view it; and the more the number of people who view it, the better your chances of being noticed and recruited.

The second way of gaining popularity is by expressing your views and posts by using LinkedIn Pulse.

LinkedIn Pulse is a platform for LinkedIn members to publish their work or thoughts and ideas for others to read and comment. It works like a blog, allowing you to post information on your field of expertise.

Through LinkedIn Pulse, you can share your insights on a specific topic of interest, and share it with the LinkedIn Community at large. You can present articles, research reports, summaries of research reports, and others on this forum. LinkedIn Pulse is also a discussion forum where the LinkedIn community can express their views on the topics that you have presented.

These articles and presentations will go a long way in helping you develop a strong brand in the community.

Wrap up

Before I move to concluding the book, I believe it will be a good idea for me to wrap up the discussions we had in this book, so that the ideas you were exposed to are reinforced.

Having identified in detail, what you need to do to search for jobs on LinkedIn, I would like to present a few tips on how to effectively search for jobs on LinkedIn.

I have pointed out most of what you need to do throughout the book, and here is a snapshot of whatever was presented over the last few chapters.

Profile

A discussed since the beginning of the book, your profile is the most important part of LinkedIn. This profile is essentially your online "resume" and you should know how to present your resume to the users of LinkedIn, including those in you network, and potential recruiters. Your aim here is to use LinkedIn to get you a job, and your profile should appropriately reflect your goal of getting a job.

Your profile must:

1. Be clear, accurate and complete, filling out all sections. You may find some sections are not applicable to you. You may request LinkedIn to skip these sections for now. For e.g. if you are a finance professional, patents may not be relevant to you.
2. Include a professional and appropriate photo
3. Include a clear professional headline: the professional title or headline is what appears when a recruiter searches for profiles. An accurate and specific profile will give you an edge over others in the site. If you are studying in a university, it is not sufficient for you to say, "Student at XXX University." Similarly, you shouldn't say too much too, like "Recent Master of Business Administration" or "Finance Executive, Global Projects Division at YYY Engineering."
4. Be set to public viewing. This means that you will appear in searches more frequently and you need to keep your profile

appropriate, accurate, and updated since the world of LinkedIn can see it.

5. Detail your education and professional experience completely but concisely: Make sure that you include details about the positions you held, as well as your responsibilities and accomplishments, not just your job titles.

6. Highlight your recent internship and training experience. Your internship or training experience adds value to your profile and gives you an edge when recruiters search for profiles.

Contacts/Connections

Connections or contacts help you to expand your virtual network of professionals. You can expand your network by searching for people you know and clicking "Connect" against their name on their profile page.

Make sure you add people you know to build up your connections. These can be friends, colleagues, classmates, former bosses or co-workers.

Also add your supervisors from your internship/training program, as connections, as well as any co-workers or fellow interns from your host employer. LinkedIn is a way to keep in touch with each of them on a professional basis. This will help you now whom your connections might know and it's helpful to see what they end up doing in their own careers.

Use the "People you may know" feature: This tool is very useful! It suggests people you may have come into contact with based on your jobs, schools, people you have emailed with, friends of friends, etc.

If someone you know appears here, invite them to connect and start a conversation. Include a personal message, a reminder of when you met them and the context of the meeting. Once you are connected, you can get a sense of whom they may be connected to. Make sure you consider this question when you connect with them. Do any of these people work in companies with which you would want to work? They could make an introduction and put you in touch with the right people at their companies.

Search through your connections and see where people are working to investigate potential employers. Consider whether these people are working in those companies that you would be interested in working. Make the first contact at the company, inquiring about possible job openings or email any current connection and see if you can get an introduction.

When adding connections, make sure you send a personal request to them. While, LinkedIn will give you a generic "Request to Connect" as text for the invitation, it's always better to put a personal touch to your message, since it will be more meaningful to the potential connection. It will also help the person to recall you at the appropriate time.

Always respond to messages and invitations in a timely manner, especially ones regarding jobs. Timing can be very crucial. You can miss out on an opportunity because you were slow in responding.

Recall something that I mentioned earlier in the book. You get what you put into LinkedIn. If you want to get the most out of it as a job search tool, you need keep yourself updated about the homepage/news of the companies you are targeting and interact with your connections regularly. If you don't respond to someone, you can't expect him or her to help you. Make sure that you give a positive impression to the people you interact with.

Don't be afraid to keep a conversation going or ask for an introduction with one of a connection's connections.

The more you develop relationships with your connections, the easier and more likely it is for them to remember you in the future, and they would want to offer their knowledge or network to you. The next time a job opens up in their company, they would want to think of you.

Groups

I have pointed out the importance of groups, and how you can join them, and contribute positively.

Join groups that are of professional interest to you so you can begin to see and connect with others with similar career fields.

These can be university alumni groups, clubs or associations, industry-specific groups, etc. Most importantly, join groups that will allow you to connect with people working in your field or industry

Never confuse "groups" with "companies." All companies/businesses are found on the **company page**. Groups can be affiliated with a company, but in general, they are separate from the company. A company can have many groups, but groups are unique.

Some groups require authentication. Keep in mind that after you request to join a group, the administrators may need to authenticate or approve you. In other words, they want to ensure that the group is right for you, and you have a genuine interest in contributing to the group.

Monitor group activity. What are people talking about? What are the buzzwords and hot topics in your chosen field/industry? Do you have anything to contribute? Many group members often post job openings that they think are relevant to the group; check the group often.

Add to discussions: Feel free to add a comment or generate a discussion of your own if you have something relevant to say. Make sure that you don't post things that are relevant only to you. Don't initiate a dialogue, such as "Can anyone get me a job here?" To be a successful networker, you need to build a relationship with a person before you inquire about opportunities.

Make connections: Connect with people who are discussing topics that are related to your field/industry. Do any of these people work at companies where you would want to pursue employment? – is a question that you need to consider whenever you are in a discussion with your connections.

Build relationships with new connections: Invite them to start a conversation and network with them. They may have valuable information about the industry of your choice, or you may have things in common to discuss with them. Consider these questions: Do you know any of these people? Or do they know others in the industry?

Companies

Many companies will create a "company page" on LinkedIn to represent themselves and build their online presence. This page is similar to the fan page you may find on Facebook, where a company generates activity, initiates discussions and shares updates.

This page allows you to see basic information about the company and people who you may currently be working there. You can also view any current job openings at the company.

You should follow companies you are interested in working. This allows you to see updates about them. If you get an interview call from any of these companies, you will have less research to do later.

You can find these company updates on the company's page or on your homepage/activity feed where you see updates about your connections.

You can also invite people at this company to connect with you and make sure that you include a personal message. Even if they are not the right person to be speaking with about current job openings, they can probably tell you whom to contact or even put you directly in touch with that person.

Recommendations and Endorsements

This feature is relatively new and can be a great way to let other LinkedIn users to know more about you. You can ask for recommendations or endorsements from colleagues, former professors or supervisors.

Give recommendations to others; remember, what goes around, comes around. So, when you recommend or endorse others, it will display your name on those users' profiles, making you more visible to potential connections.

Research
Use LinkedIn to find out information about people before you meet them or have an interview with them

If you know about the person you would be meeting at the company beforehand, it will always come in handy. Make sure that you do not to make it obvious during the interview that you know specific details about them. You may give the impression that you were cyber stalking them.

Use "Company Pages" to see who of your connections works at a particular company, if you have any connections in common with someone who works there or if anyone at the company is in your extended network.

Network
LinkedIn is a **great networking tool,** so don't be afraid to use it as such.

You can connect with people you don't know and build a strong relationship. Reach out to people who may be able to assist you in your job search. Even if they can't assist you, they may know someone who can.

In addition, you can do the following to catch the attention of potential recruiters.

You can start a conversation with someone in one of your groups: Consider what do you have in common? Maybe, you attended the same university or know some common connections. Or perhaps they previously worked in a company where you would like to join and they can put you in touch with the right person in the company.

Ask questions: People love to talk about themselves. When you invite someone to connect, ask them something. It can be anything from how they got involved in the field or a question about a specific aspect of their profile, such as a previous job or particular project. The key is to find the "links" between you and the other person to generate a discussion. When you ask a question, the other person is forced to ask you a question too. Thus, you have shared your backgrounds and career interests with each other.

Don't get discouraged and stay positive: Don't be offended if someone doesn't accept your invitation to connect, doesn't respond to a message or doesn't ask a question about you in return. People use LinkedIn differently, some check it every day and others use it sporadically. If you don't hear back from someone, just let it go and work with the connections you do have.

Use your access to a wider pool of connections: It's important to keep in mind that once you connect with someone, you are getting access to a large pool of potential connections, so I suggest that you take advantage of this wider pool of connections. When you click on someone's profile you are not connected with, you can see the common connections and the degree of separation between the two of you. While some connects cannot assist you, others may. This is how you will work with the professionals in your network to assist you in your job search.

What goes out comes back: LinkedIn should be mutually beneficial. If someone helps you or puts you in touch with someone, thank him or her! Likewise, if they ask a favor of you or even send you a message, respond to them promptly and/or return the favor if you can. Even if they can't help you at this time, you should still be responsive and courteous to all of your connections because you never know when that could change.

News & Updates
Stay on top of the news in your industry: Monitor companies you are interested in to see what's new with them or if they have posted any new positions.

Check your feed regularly: This will show you who has been promoted, changed jobs, etc., which means they may now be working for a company or in a field that interests you.

Reach out to connections with relevant news: You can share an industry-related article that you find interesting to let your connection know you thought of them or you can congratulate them on a promotion. Fostering networking relationships is crucial because you not only learn from each other but also help each other in search of employment and career development.

Jobs

The "Jobs" section of the site may seem like the most obvious place to find a job using LinkedIn, but it's just as important to maintain a solid group of connections; join groups and stay up-to-date with companies' news.

In order to search for a job, go to the Jobs page and perform a standard search. You can search by keyword, job title or company; and you can save searches to come back to at a later time.

The Advanced Search area allows you to narrow your search even further

- You can search by your country, industry and even job function.
- Make sure to search by your country so you only see positions relevant to your location.
- Utilize the location feature, so you can search in your city and/or surrounding area (i.e. Hong Kong) and not just the entire country (i.e. China).
- Unfortunately, you have to pay to upgrade your LinkedIn account to "Job Seeker Premium" if you want to search by salary and have access to other features of the job listings.

Email alerts: You can set up email alerts so you receive emails if a job has been posted to LinkedIn that meets your search criteria. The "Jobs You May Be Interested In" section of the "Jobs" page will populate with the listings that you think will be relevant based on your profile and preferences. You can then,

⇨ Save a Job: You can "save" a job you are interested in at any time by doing one of the following:
⇨ Click "Save job" when it appears as you move your mouse over a job in the Jobs search results.
⇨ Click the star icon that appears as you move your mouse over a job in the "Jobs You May Be Interested In" section.
⇨ Click the "Save job" link in the top right of a job posting under the "Apply" button.

You can see jobs you've saved or already applied to at any time by clicking "Jobs" at the top of your homepage and clicking "Saved jobs" in the right-hand column.

For more information, you can register for a LinkedIn Webinar, especially the Job Search Webinar: The Job Search Webinar is free. Finally, you can check the LinkedIn Blog for job search tips and tricks, given at the bottom of the page.

You can find more information about the Webinar, blog and any other information in the Help Centre Page of www.linkedin.com.

Chapter 17 – Conclusion

Well friends, you have a lot of work to do now. If you are searching for a job, the right time to use LinkedIn was months ago, or probably a year ago.

Remember, getting a job through LinkedIn will take time, and you need to have loads of patience to get one. You will need to build your network, your referrals, your recommendations and your endorsements. You will have to reciprocate these by referring others, recommending and endorsing them for what they are.

You may ask, what is the big deal when there are so many job portals that can get me a job quickly? You need to understand that the focus of most job portals is on you, as an individual. You need to highlight "your" achievements, skills and experience, and everything related to you.

While you do highlight these in your LinkedIn Profile, your focus is not about advertising your achievements and credentials. Your focus is to get people to network with you, and people will network with you only when you are willing to bow down and make others feel important.

Remove the focus from "I". Focus on them, how you can help them, solve their problems, and be of value to them. When you become of value to others, they will be more than willing to help you.

LinkedIn is harnessing the power of the Internet to help you capitalize on your connections' connections, their connections, their connections' connections… and so on. This is the power of multiplication, or exponentiation.

If you have 10 connections, and each of the 10 connections have 10 other connections, potentially, you can connect to 10 x 10 = 100 connections. Now, these 100 connections have 10 connections each, you potentially have connections to 1000 people. Isn't it great to have

1000 connections, and you are able to connect with each of them and get to know them, personally and professionally.

These 1000 connections would come from every corners of the world, various fields of life, occupation and educational background.

You, as an individual, will not only grow professionally, but also personally, because you get to know a large group of individuals, and they will be able to vouch for you when the time comes, and can help you get a job too.

One important point I would like to clarify here is this. Never make it obvious to others that you are seeking a job. Seeking a job is the byproduct of being in the network. Your sole focus of being a member of LinkedIn is to create and expand your professional network.

As part of expanding your professional network, you are required to be proactive, follow what people and companies in their respective profile pages, contribute to the discussion, provide valuable insights, and convey your thought leadership by publishing articles, start discussion forums and share documents that would be of interest to others.

LinkedIn purchased SlideShare in 2012. SlideShare is a platform for you to showcase your talent and thought leadership by publishing articles, documents, presentations and videos to your followers. The more the number of followers you have, the better your chances are for getting recognized and recruited.

By focusing on your network, you can land in the job of your choice, and you will require loads of patience. You need to have a balance between focus on you as well as on your network.

Undue focus on your network without focusing on your achievements will lead you to nowhere. You definitely want your colleagues and people in your network to endorse you for the skills that you bring to the table. And for your colleagues to endorse and refer you, you need to prove your worth in your current organization.

This will require you to keep updating your profile every now and then, with information related to your promotion, your achievements, successful completion of projects, new patents that you have been awarded with, certificate courses that you may have attended, and many others.

These updates will definitely attract the attention of recruiters and if you are smart enough, you will update them to reflect your utility value to these recruiters.

To cut the long story short, maintain a balance between what you do and your focus on people in your network. Have loads of patience, and be active in your network. You are sure to land a job in the company or industry of your choice and you will reap the benefits of LinkedIn.

Before I conclude, I would also like to issue a word of caution. Never stop your activities on LinkedIn after you have got a job. Once you have got a job, it is all the more important for you to be in touch with the ones who helped you get the job. If you do not, you are seen as a self-serving individual, who resorted to glib talk when you were in need of a job and left people high and dry when they needed your reference and recommendation.

All the best for your job search and I truly believe LinkedIn will help you achieve your goal of working for the company you have always dreamt.

www.ingramcontent.com/pod-product-compliance
Lightning Source LLC
Chambersburg PA
CBHW071838200526
45169CB00020B/1820

* 9 781530 604647 *